WITH A POET'S EYE

With a Poet's Eye

A TATE GALLERY ANTHOLOGY

edited by Pat Adams

THE TATE GALLERY

FRONT COVER
Thomas Girtin, *The White House at Chelsea*
1800, (detail)

Photograph of Tate Gallery by A. Williams

ISBN 0 946590 38 9 (paper)
ISBN 0 946590 39 7 (cloth)
Published by order of the Trustees 1986
Designed by Caroline Johnston
Published by Tate Gallery Publications,
Millbank, London SW1P 4RG
Printed by Balding + Mansell Limited,
Wisbech, Cambs

Foreword

It is a particular pleasure for us to publish this anthology, 'With a Poet's Eye'. All these poems whether by authors established or unknown, are new, and all are inspired by paintings and sculptures in the Tate Gallery.

The anthology is the culmination of a year of activities at the Gallery when we have sought to explore the relationships between poetry and the visual arts. Readings and workshops were followed by a Poetry Competition which was far more successful than we had ever hoped to expect. The best entries, by children as well as by adults, are included in this eye-opening volume, together with poems which were specially invited. For everyone involved this has been a most exciting and gratifying time, and I would like to offer the Gallery's thanks to all those who have responded and helped us. All our participants would, I am sure, wish to join me in expressing a particular gratitude to Pat Adams of the Gallery's Education Department. She makes her own acknowledgements on page 6, but everyone knows that what became an art and poetry festival was her idea and her responsibility. This volume that she has edited, 'With a Poet's Eye', is assuredly going to give long and lasting pleasure to generations of gallery visitors.

ALAN BOWNESS *Director*

Acknowledgements

Writing to a specific theme is not always easy and we were surprised and heartened by the warm reaction of the poets we approached: we are grateful to them all, not least to those who wanted to contribute but for whom, on this occasion, the Muse's inspired influence was unforthcoming.

In the preparation of the anthology itself we are exceptionally grateful to Henry Moore for his kind permission to reproduce 'Seated Woman, 1970-1' and to Bruce McLean for provision of and permission to reproduce a colour study for 'Construction of the Grey Flag'. I owe much to the friendship and encouragement of Dannie and Joan Abse who, having themselves already begun to compile a similar collection of poems and pictures, were always ready to give me their time and the opportunity to discuss and exchange ideas. We are particularly grateful to Kevin Crossley-Holland who has brought the anthology to a much wider audience, through his series of 'Time for Verse' programmes on BBC Radio 4.

The Tate Gallery 1985 Poetry Competition, from which the idea for the anthology sprang, secured the enthusiastic help and support of many people. For their valuable advice in the initial stages of organising the competition we are grateful to Brian Mitchell and Michelle Fink at the Poetry Society and to Jonathan Barker and Jennifer Insull at the Arts Council Poetry Library. We are indebted to the judges Fleur Adcock, Alan Brownjohn, Gillian Clarke, Gavin Ewart and Gareth Owen for undertaking the laborious process of selection. Likewise we are grateful to IBM United Kingdom Trust, Reader's Digest Association Ltd, Thames & Hudson and Winsor & Newton for their generous provision of prizes. Among those who liberally gave many hours of their own time I would particularly like to thank schoolteachers Angela Humphries and Cilla Murrin for preliminarily sifting the children's entries.

Finally I would like to extend my thanks to all those in the Tate who have helped me in a variety of ways and especially Simon Wilson and my colleagues in the Education Department for their consideration and support throughout the past eventful year.

PAT ADAMS

Introduction

'. . . I live in the eye: and my imagination, surpassed, is at rest . . .'
John Keats – Letter to Thomas Keats 27 June 1818

Less than a minute is usually the most that is given to works of art encountered on a gallery visit. To extend this fleeting glance into something more prolonged and reflective has long been the ambition of gallery curators the world over. This ambition was pursued by the Tate Gallery in 1985 when it ran a series of events linking art with poetry. These included a national poetry competition for all ages and poetry workshops for children and adults: a series of lunchtime readings of their work in the galleries, given by distinguished poets, brought alive Horace's *ut pictura poesis* (as with the painter's work so with the poet's). The production of an illustrated anthology of poems, to be written by leading contemporary poets, seemed the natural sequel to these events. However at the time when poets were invited to contribute it was impossible to predict their virtually unanimous acceptance or the richness of their response.

This selection, from the abundance of commissioned poems which finally reached us, also includes some of the winning entries from both the adult and children's sections of the open competition. The poems it presents are those in which the subject, either an individual work of art or some aspect of the Gallery itself, has been the stimulus to more than poetical description. In them the poet, through a personal vision and expression, brings to the subject a wider, sometimes entirely unexpected dimension, which in turn evokes new visual images. Quite simply they are the poems which most encouraged us to return to look afresh at the works which inspired them.

The poems are arranged more or less in the order in which their subjects would be found if the reader were to make a chronological tour of the Gallery. The subjects are fairly evenly distributed between the Tate's Historic British

Collection and Modern Collection, the division between them being marked by a poem on Auguste Rodin's 'The Muse'. Occasionally instances occur where two poems are associated with the same work: where this happens the contrast in their author's approach to the subject vividly illustrates the capacity inherent in a work of art to elicit an entirely personal response. The presence of three poems, selected from a score or more, on works by Francis Bacon, reflects the impact of the major exhibition of that artist's work held at the Tate Gallery during 1985.

Nearly every poem is accompanied by a colour reproduction of the work which attracted its author. Naturally the richest experience will be gained from reading the poems in the presence of the originals where qualities such as texture and scale will further contribute to the way in which the reader's sensibility is affected.

The completion of this poetic tour will underline our gratitude to the poets who have made it possible: they will have widened our perceptions of the Gallery and this small selection of the works it houses. Much more, both at the Tate and in other museums and galleries is worthy of similar discovery. Recalling the responses in this anthology we may eventually find it becomes second nature to devote more time to individual works and to reflect upon them with a poet's eye.

Contents

The Tate Gallery

ELIZABETH JENNINGS

I

Preen no prejudice, but saunter into this proud building,
Remove your hat. Let your bags and baskets be examined
For bomb and gun.
Though within there will be blasts and explosions,
Important blows, battles and fisticuffs
With the history of art, for here are no concessions, no unsuitable reticence,
Be ready to be shaken, to toss out your inhibitions. Take off dark and pink glasses,
Unarmoured stand and reflect on improbable landscapes,
That easy scenery, coherent colours
Are out of court. Here is a kingdom of trial and error. Experiment
Is Emperor and everywhere a lively court is kept under soft control,
Allowed out on excursions, sent for on search-parties and reconnaissance,
Ambassadors and envoys are on the look-out for empirical makers,
Avoiding valleys, scaling stark mountains, hurrying, never at rest.
And you walk here with a ticket of freedom, a pass to dangerous escarpments,
The guards here are wary of withdrawals,
Will watch you watching canvas and metal, stone and clay,
A country then where Nature is often bypassed,
    where rocks are hacked and broken, borders
    footstepped and trampled,
But remember what is wanted from you is a good giving,
A generous benefaction – your open ideas,
    your wide mind with its gates flung
    back and windows open.
You will be received here by international personages,
Reclaimers, responders, builders, lavish spenders,

Rothko, Ernst, Magritte and Modigliani,
But Blake will restore your confidence,
Palmer hold out his hand.
Come, enter, accept this gilt-edged invitation,
You are important and needed. Your gaze is urgent,
Watch Turner bonfire the sky,
You are wanted for these lavish pyrotechnics.

THE TATE GALLERY

II

Think of these at night when no-one sees
The fearful summons and unsparing brush.
Ernst is a haunter with dark images.

Imagine ghosts of gazers seeing flesh
Hinted at. Rodin is there of course,
Yet in a night-time gallery, the wish

Of all past lookers and their live discourse
Might haunt the air. 'Here,' one might say, 'My dread
Is captured. I've had dreams like that, a curse

On easy sleeping'. Do these painters then
Darken our day to help us through the night
Knowing that we are scared and little men?

Perhaps, but we are ones who climb to bright
Precarious moments, love those abstract lines
Of Nicholson and Mondrian. Our sight

Is sharpened in this place of many signs
Directing us within but also out
To how the sky behaves or moon reclines.

The Tate's pure purpose cannot be in doubt.

III

Place of mirror and mirage, hint, retirement and then
Sudden fierce arrivals, after shunting in sidings, of paintings which have unloaded
Influence, bias, and bring in their own views of now, visions of time beyond us almost, also
Warhol, Pollock, Hockney, all, in a way, shockers, shapers of work
Which affronts us, takes us by the scruff, giddys us to come round and stand, shakily still
Before the risk and rise of intemperate choices, blatant colours, bearers
Almost, of ungrace. And yet, and yet . . . look closer,
Dare to stare at the tricks played by Magritte, be willing to admit
That painters had to leap down unconscious minds, and
Out-Freud Freud, healing not by talking trouble away, but by being forced
To admit art must go this way, find a difficult sturdy beauty in all unlikeliness,
And, as a touchstone, stare at Blake or Palmer,
Open your eyes to your own mind reflected
But improved, given form and purpose,
Painted out of the colour-box of the rainbow,
Shocking us only to save us for this moment
In an age at ease with violence and terror.
An almost impossible peace may here be gathered,
But has to be won by a courage of total looking.

Magical Mystery Tour

GAVIN EWART

PART ONE

Surely I remember?
The coach that took the Sixth Formers
to see the Blakes and the Impressionists and the Post-Impressionists
and the Cubists, and the sculpture of Rodin?
Van Gogh's chair, Modigliani's wonderful peasant boy,
Beatrice addressing the Likely Lads from the car,
the Simoniac Pope?
Surely, I remember.

Fifty years ago!
And now I go back to see The Ghost of a Flea
so well remembered, and The Man Who Built the Pyramids
(forgotten – if seen) and James Ward's Gordale Scar
and Maillol's three nymphs with identical leg-lengths
and a marvellous sunstruck outburst of Turners,
all as potent
as fifty years ago.

PART TWO

But there's a lot new there, to see,
and in Nineteen boxed-in Thirty Three
they'd have blushed red to know
such a pubic Delvaux
and the sculpture would quite spoil their tea –

while one painting, The Sword Of The Pig,
shows in detail what leaves of a fig
were once much used to hide
(though Blake's drawings tried) –
a male organ quite lifesize and big!

And McWilliam. His Eye, Nose and Cheek
would have boggled the minds of the meek
who were after Burne-Jones
and his temperate zones
(*not* Picasso, that two-faced old freak!),

likewise Warhol's repeated Monroe,
Arman's shaving brush Venus, would go
near to making them mad,
and they'd surely be glad
to leave Lichtenstein – WHAM! BAM! what woe!

They'd be mystified, as by George Smiley,
by the abstract arcane Bridget Riley –
and go straight as an arrow
to the construct by Caro?
I don't think so. Though *we* rate them highly.

Still there's the trompe l'oeil fresco/frieze
where in past years they served all the teas,
Rex Whistler's pastiche!
Now it's red wine and quiche –
but the whole lot is what you *can't* please!

AUTHOR'S NOTE PAGE 156

The Saltonstall Family

JUDITH KAZANTZIS

The strangest family portrait I ever saw.
Six members: two children, a baby
a man and two women compose it.
Two children on the left
link hands to a troubled father
whose free hand, in a white glove
hooks back a rich chrysanthemum red
stage curtain; in fact a bed curtain.

Behind these folds and his golden
doublet and their red brocaded
dresses lies the mother, slack mouthed
and shroud faced as the ghost
she was by the year the artist came.
And to the right hand front –
decorously she holds her own infant,
the stepmother, the second wife.

The stepmother of the children
sits in a castle of satin, fold
building on fold. Her young
ringletted face guards sincere
duty done, pride and unease.
Her boy is bound like a dahlia
bud in red and gold. She's
model for a stepdaughter, bride white.

DAVID DES GRANGES
The Saltonstall Family

The mother dying looks with eyes
dark, bright, detached – delirious?
back at her little pair. She stares
round her husband, too far gone
to be sincere; just stares. Out of
her time, dazed. Once more
she empties her cumbrous fingers
to bless, to give him those lives.

So I'm circled back to see how
his own linked hand ushers these
children across to the second wife.
He looks at her across the inset
phantom – How to interpret this
look? Sensual, or proud or grateful?
Or, his eyebrows delicate under
the crowned hat and the massed hair,

a withdrawn relief at sincere duty
done? In any event his gaze
travels out past the woman,
I see now. And I am angry at how
this man, in his domestic love,
grew master of sad histories
manager of life, and death and births
his players growing devout or dead.

And also happy. See the child
the older one. Leaning, swaying
she gazes straight (the only one)
at our naive and honest painter
Master Des Granges, who's weaving a
pretty idyll to keep her still.

She's bursting with giggles and 'Sir
I shan't believe you!' There, dancing

she stands, pursemouthed and brilliant
eyed, holding her father's hand.

*   *   *

Except, I've made a mistake.
This vivid 'girl' is a boy really
in petticoats still but, look,
no apron. Unlike the small sister
stout, stoic and white bibbed,
held quiet at this brother's hand.

So now this boy, swaying
and brilliant-eyed: he requires
another story altogether.
Des Granges leaves the dance of Flora
to thunder of bat-eyed monsters
and wars. 'I'll slay you dragons!'
the boy calls out his shining
promise, holding his father's hand.

As for the girl with no apron,
who was my own ghost in a family
portrait spooky with right habit,
she tries to exist after all.
Her form shining under the boy's.
A possibility interred.
And she is the saddest ghost truth of
her mother, unpainted, unheard of.

AUTHOR'S NOTE PAGE 160

Homage to George Stubbs

JOHN HEATH-STUBBS

I claim no kinship with this Cheshire man:
My forebears were of Staffordshire, at least
Since Charles the Martyr's time. But Stubbs
Is a good north west midlands name, and if you traced
The bloodstreams further back, it's like enough
You'd find they would converge. But may I hazard
A fellowship of spirit with him, son of a groom,
Who hung up from the rafters the lifeless body of a horse –
Such as his father had fondled, currycombed, and cosseted
With hot bran mash, and children brought their gifts to –
Apples and sugar-lumps? Scalpel, knife, and saw,
Scraped, carved, and bit, slicing the mighty sinews.
The convolutions of the bowels unwound;
The heart displayed its secret chambers, and the brain
Was lifted from its citadel, the skull, until at length
Only the white and chalky bones remained. Commitment thus
Behoves, to stinking fact, if we would enter
That clearing in the forest of the mind
Where animal energies, equine and leonine,
Engage each other with great uncleft hoof,
With gleaming tooth, and ripping, savage talon.

GEORGE STUBBS
Horse attacked by a Lion

Sir Brooke Boothby

GERDA MAYER

Sir Brooke, reclining by a brook,
How punningly your lines flow
Beside your namesake. Time has changed
The leaves to autumn overhead.
You clasp Rousseau.

And all your nature's heraldry
Is here set out. It is your look –
Voluptuous, thoughtful, quizzical,
Has puzzled me for many years,
Beloved Sir Brooke.

Two years ago they cleaned you up.
Still sensuous, you leer the less;
No longer the seducer but
Hinting of sorrows yet to come,
And pensiveness.

Yet still amused, – you scrutinise
Me as intently as I you.
Dumpy and old, I've fared the worse.
Will others come when I am gone,
Or be as true?

My very sparkling Brooke, we are
Two centuries and Styx apart.
Yet mirror-imaged our loss

(Your child, my father) and we share
A love for art.

It would be pleasant if we were
Among the leaves so juxtaposed –
You on the left, I on the right –
That you would flow above me when
The book was closed.

AUTHOR'S NOTE PAGE 1 6 1

JOSEPH WRIGHT OF DERBY
Sir Brooke Boothby

Henry Fuseli: 'Titania and Bottom'

PETER SCUPHAM

Out of your cold dream, Mr Fuseli,
Where reason slept and monsters were begotten,
Come iced flesh, these bluish night-sweats,

Catafalques of hair, teasings-out of ribbon:
Nymphs and lamias of the demi-monde
Whose tarnished features ghost this bedchamber.

Nel mezzo del cammin – the dark sheets ruck
Where the ground heaves, and a hidden moon
Plays limbo's midwife, addling the narrow wits

Of Brother Ass, hunched on his coarse throne,
Feeling the brute stir in his cruel member:
A rustic Midas, flowering into godhead

And moving grandly to his jovial climax.
Light patches faces on a wall of leaves,
Flows down the pliant limbs, a branchwork

Whose draperies are less than a first snowfall,
The mere congealing of high-summer shadow.
A smile buries its thorn in that hot flesh

Which the bright dews will search and scarify
Upon the stained floor of a wood near nowhere:
Her crooked thread woven into his broadcloth.

HENRY FUSELI
Titania and Bottom

God Creating Adam

D.J. ENRIGHT

Either He is fatigued –
Creation takes it out of you
And this is the sixth day –
Or else He is having second thoughts.
(But God's first are always right.)

Adam has no thoughts at the moment,
Only a certain bewilderment:
It was all so sudden,
There's no substitute for a leisurely womb.

He hardly seems a sufficient abyss
To be so intensely brooded over.
How can he hope to live up to it?

The serpent is already coiled about him.
Surely a premature appearance?
(Though no surprise to the Omniscient.)

Heretics would say later, it was life
Snaking out of Adam's right foot –
As if He'd left a hole in it!
Or perhaps intended, Eve as yet undreamt of,
For a household pet. Snakes have clean habits.

Prudently God provides Adam with ribs in plenty:
No need to start from scratch next time.
'I must create a system,' He is thinking,
'And leave the rest to them . . .'
The snake is whispering about a thing called 'sex',
Though what it is he doesn't know from Adam.

Can that really be the sunset –
Louring and chaotic?
It doesn't look natural,
Not exactly the shepherd's delight.

Next there would have to be a Shepherd.
That's the trouble with creating,
There's no end to it.

WILLIAM BLAKE
Elohim creating Adam

The Elohim

ROY FISHER

Blake drew the guilt of God,
showed him at his compulsion
in plain view; past the moment
of holding back and not
forcing the universe
to break into matter from the void;

by the very act obliged
for a while to be
imaginable, all the world
hurrying into being
and looking on.

Blake, on behalf of Adam,
put the secret question everybody has:

'How was it, that particular minute
when I was made?'

And stained Eternity
with common answers. 'Troubled.
At cross-purposes. Recklessly aware
as to consequence. Streaked through
with the sense of something
suddenly and forever lost'.

Nebuchadnezzar

COLIN ARCHER

He goes missing again, this beast of a thing
Inherited from Blake (who got him
From God knows where) – and I cannot rest
Until I check he is safely back.

He always hears me enter, knows
I will come straight to his glass quarantine –
For I swear he is almost human
As he stares at me, appalled and appalling.

If I turn away, he howls,
Invents some escape, leaps out at me,
Demands the lead, and like some mad guide dog
Hurtles me to his own destinations.

I hold my end gladly at first
For in this place sight is not enough
And he alone has the sense and license
To slobber paint, worry the sculpture.

He sniffs out Gwen John, remembering
The fine bones she barely bothers to hide,
And the taut leather binding us
Transmits the thrills of his nostrils to my brain.

Nebuchadnezzar is ripe today –
Rubs up against Stubbs, shamelessly races me
To Dame Barbara, reclining,
Tongues the orifice, mounts her.

I break them apart, and his frustrated energy
Drags me to every last lamp-post
In Salford, to Chelsea, and on to Cookham
Where he ups the swans.

Distracted by some high call
Far beyond any human register,
He stops short, delicately nosing the excrement
Of the recently arrived.

WILLIAM BLAKE
Nebuchadnezzar

This is more than I can take in one day –
Grab at his verminous hair
To shake the living daylights into him
As I head through the revolving door.

But he will not let me go, moves in on me
To dog my days, disturb my nights,
Disappears again, leaving only his stare
Scorched here on my white paint.

Samuel Palmer's
'Coming from Evening Church'

CHARLES CAUSLEY

The heaven-reflecting, usual moon
Scarred by thin branches, flows between
The simple sky, its light half-gone,
The evening hills of risen green.
Safely below the mountain crest
A little clench of sheep holds fast.
The lean spire hovers like a mast
Over its hulk of leaves and moss
And those who, locked within a dream,
Make between church and cot their way
Beside the secret-springing stream
That turns towards an unknown sea;
And there is neither night nor day,
Sorrow nor pain, eternally.

SAMUEL PALMER
Coming from Evening Church

The Shipwreck

JOHN WAIN

This canvas yells the fury of the sea.
Across a quiet room, where people murmur
their poised appreciations, it shrieks out
the madness of the wind.
                              How can that be?
Woven of voiceless threads, its pigments laid
with 'no more sound than the mice make', it hurls
the tempest at my eardrums, and my eyes
smart in the lashing spray. But not before
the colours of tragedy have enkindled them:
it must be so, because the colours hold
the secret. They are noise, and tilt, and steepness.
The colours are trough, and crash, the cry of gulls
lifted and blown away like part of the spume.
The colours are the bawling of the wind.
That yellow sail, its mast snapped sideways, catches
into itself and holds that gleam of light
amid the livid waters, the evening gleam
through torn black cloud as the sullen day departs.
One last message of life. Over and out.
The people in the small escaping boat
(too frail for the uncaring slide and smash
of those tall water-cliffs, promising only
ten minutes more of life, of clinging on

J.M.W. TURNER
The Shipwreck

before the toppling plunge) see in that yellow
the last of life that they will ever see.
A goodbye signal, perhaps a welcoming
to those new neighbours, whoever they will be,
who wait for them on the other side of darkness,
below the clap of the waves and lace of foam
down there in the dark, and then below the dark,
in the calm of the still depths (the most tremendous
storm makes no disturbance below nine fathoms).
Will their new world be down on the ocean-floor,
among the caves? Or, following the blown gulls,
through some still gleaming crevice of the sky?
Or will they start again on the green earth,
as newts this time, or leaning-tower giraffes,
or crocodiles who lie still as old tyres
in estuary mud? Or human children
with different facial bones and frizzy hair?
Or will they be the atoms of the water
next time, and hammer some trim ketch to planks
and floating spars? Will they be starfish, lying
five-pointed on the beach these voyagers
would give, in this death-minute, everything
they ever owned to be treading, calmly, now?
Who knows? What we can ask, I think, is
whether death will seem beautiful to them when it comes,
and to us, for that matter, after the pain

is over, I mean. Many great artists have
extolled the beauty of death, have loved and called to it,
and Turner here seems to be saying *Now
I will show you how terror and agony
and the utterly final arrival of death can distil
an essence of beauty-in-terror, an enrichment
in the moment of final relinquishment of all*:
as if it took that knowledge, that edge of torment,
to peel away the cataract from our vision,
to reveal the beauty of those mad waters
and that last gleam of light from a hostile day.
Meanwhile, one thing I know: the silent canvas
has stored the howl and thunder of that hour,
the yell of death in the ears of the sacrificed:
the last groan of the timbers, the frantic slap
of the saturated sail. Canvas to canvas. Sound
to silence, through the artist's compassionate mind,
and back to sound again, as I stand here.

Oh, it has 'painterly values' too, and can be discussed
in purely abstract terms: but not now, not now.
Some other time, not in the presence of
the human creatures, air-breathers, gulping their last,
and the sea's roaring that never will be quenched,
and beyond, the starfish at his supine vigil
on the final beach whose shingle we shall be.

Yacht Approaching the Coast

PATRICIA BEER

Winds ago the Gordons' yacht
Approached a coast of lemon sand,
Long hills with rivers sliding out.
It was just as they had planned,
The details sharp as glass, clear cut:

City women who had left home
For a month to walk beside the ocean
And past the new assembly room,
Parasols opening to the sun,
Pugs breathing like a well-bred dream,

The villas in their avenues
Strewn against noise with grey-green leaves
Fallen from eucalyptus trees,
The church with a design of graves
And steady angels in the grass.

Where suddenly the tide-race shivers
They took their pick of the white houses
And near the safest of the rivers
In my home town of all places
Sat down beside the other rovers.

But on goes Turner's sailing boat
Through the scarlet whirlpool (past
The Gordons sitting dressed in white)
Dancing, to join an unquiet coast
That he can see and they could not.

J.M.W. TURNER
Yacht Approaching the Coast

JOHN CROME
The Poringland Oak

The Long and Lovely Summers

VERNON SCANNELL

How long and lovely were the summers then,
Each misted morning verdant milk, until
The sun blurred through, at first a pallid wen
Beneath the sky's bland skin and then, still pale,
A swollen, silvery dahlia-head, before
It burned to gold on laundered gentian blue.

At noon the picnic by the waterfall,
The bright behaviour of the butterflies
Interpreting the light; the plover's call
Above the rhyming flowers, the sun-baked pies
Of cow-pats, fossilized, antique; the cool
Shades of chestnuts, little pools of night.

Night: frosted mathematics of the stars;
Homages of fragrances; the moon,
Curved kukri-blade of ice; the green guitars
And soft soprano breeze conspired to croon
Late lullabies that soothed us into dream
And on to dawn which new delights would spice.

Things are different now. The seasons mock
What expectations we may entertain.
No, things are not like that – and, taking stock,
It seems they never were. Did not grey rain
Stop play? Storms follow drought? A child was drowned.
In close-up, river nymphs were coarse and fat.

And yet we still remember them – the long
And lovely summers, never smeared or chilled –
Like poems, by heart; like poems, never wrong;
The idyll is intact, its truth distilled
From maculate fact, preserved as by the sharp
And merciful mendacities of art.

J.M.W. TURNER
The Thames near Walton Bridges

An Amateur Watercolourist to Thomas Girtin

JOHN MOLE

Your White House catches the post
From its numinous hinterland
To remind me, although I still boast
A watery brush in my hand,
That the world has gone penny-plain
Since I set out with so much hope
For those first strokes smudged by rain
On the back of an envelope.

THOMAS GIRTIN
The White House

In 'The Garden Tent'

KEVIN CROSSLEY-HOLLAND

What rhymes with aeolian chimes, swaying guardian trees?
Home sweet home, between-times, afternoons at ease.

What rhymes with this turquoise-striped, faded awning?
The sagging oak-canopy, the shaded nave yawning.

Two girls in crinoline: haircomb, bustle, stay?
White water gliding, the trill of light at play.

And, in their hands, *Persuasion? The Lady of Shalott?*
Am I locked in a dream and is time running out?

Then the snake Doubt advances, hissing 'yes and yes'.
The perfect rhymes canker in Churchyard's paradise.

THOMAS CHURCHYARD
The Garden Tent

James Ward's 'Gordale Scar'

DAVID WRIGHT

It's not a painting but a celebration,
This canvas, which seems huger than the room
It broods in, pastoral yet sybilline:
These hanging cliffs and brown romantic shades,
Darkness composed, and solitude imaged.

As for its subject – Upon the high limestone
Moors above Settle, you'll find Gordale Scar
Deflated, an authentic diminution
Of the assertion of its picture here:
The gloom is not the mood, the scale is smaller.

No reality but in imagination:
The painting is more real than the place;
More than the thing is its interpretation,
Or than its interpreter, whose bias
Of feeling, here contained, transmutes to vision.

JAMES WARD
Gordale Scar

The Deluge

AMRYL JOHNSON

No sun sets like this one
blood red eye of judgment
closing blank against the horror
shutting hard against the ruin
where frenzied limbs
snatch
at little more than hope
Spilled lives
swept away by an arc of the wrist
which wipes the page clean
almost
And the swirling devouring agent
of death
once waters of life
baptismal order
is tempered only by the artist's brush
which strokes a fevered reasoning
Fine lines angled before the tide
turned within a whirlwind of thought
to shape an anger
and seal a vast web of stillness
which churns the senses
One ray of hope trapped
the despair of wings
powerless beneath the power
of an inflexible will

draw life from the body

So
framed only in time
clutching no corners of control
save the edges of a canvas
the deluge sweeps on
through the centuries
while the I of judgment
sits firm
upon the rock
of reason

FRANCIS DANBY
The Deluge

The Boyhood of Raleigh

ALAN BROWNJOHN

But the end of it all was a shuffling line of ten thousand
Stretched out at the airport, everyone in search
Of a difference not too discomposing:
A compatible sort of bathing, docile fauna
Trotting up to nuzzle on the hotel steps,
A wheel of chance where every player wins . . .
'And when we were there it felt easy to be there,
And now we are back it feels truthful to say
"I don't feel I'm back" or "I don't feel I ever went",
The place was an illusion. We were not illusions ourselves,
We made the links between what you call "different" places,
Which are more the same because we have left our impression,
Which modifies the place as one wave modifies a beach,
Or "like" another English changes your own.
We sit with the arm of our traveller's tale extended,
Reciting the fictions of distance, we tip up our bags
And find the fools' gold of unchangeable coins,
The centimes, the bani, and here in the bottom
An unused token for a locker in Central Station,
We'll use it next time. And the children are amazed,
The boys want to go when they are adults, or when they
        have passports,

They have sat long enough being just themselves
On this side of the sea, can't they be it on the other side as well?
"Look at this!" they would like to say, holding up
The plunders of the gift shop. "You see, you see!
It proves we have been there and thought of you.
We weren't alarmed by the difference at all.
It was so immense we have brought back part of it
To be found nowhere else but there (and Victoria Station):
A duty free ballpoint pen with a toucan's head".'
What one boy thought and wrote in the room beyond
The gift shop and the green channel was
A distant recollection, of himself. All his words
Lay silent in the books, the forests continued
To grow without him, and the plundered chests of coins
Closed their lids as if he had never brought any back.
The wheel had turned and turned and stopped there.
He had gone no farther than his heart had sent him
On its regular missions of circulation.

J.E. MILLAIS
The Boyhood of Raleigh

The Boyhood of Raleigh

ROGER MCGOUGH

Entranced, he listens to salty tales
Of derring-do and giant whales,

Uncharted seas and Spanish gold,
Tempests raging, pirates bold.

And his friend? 'God I'm bored.
As for Jolly Jack, I don't believe a word.

What a way to spend the afternoons,
The stink of fish, and those ghastly pantaloons!'

The Doctor

U.A. FANTHORPE

'That Jackson, he's another one.
If he goes on opening windows we'll all
Die of pneumonia.'
              The native obsessions:
Health and the weather. Attendants have
The dogged, grainy look of subjects. Someone,
Surely, is going to paint them?

'You don't have a bad heart yet, do you?'
'Not that I know of.'
              'They can examine you.'
'But they don't really know.'

              The painters knew.
Gainsborough eyed his lovely, delicate daughters
And rich fat brewers: Turner his hectic skies.
They brooded on death by drowning (Ophelia, in real water);
Cloud without end; storm; storm coming on;
Bright exophthalmic eyes, consumptive colours,
And gorgeous goitred throats; the deluge,
The end of the world, and Adam's
Appalling worm-wrapped birth.

Such patient watchers
Have eyes for those who watch. The child
Frets in its fever, the parents
Grieve in the background gloom. But the doctor,
Who has done all he can, and knows nothing
Will help or heal, sits raptly, raptly,
As if such absorbed attention were in itself
A virtue. As it is.

LUKE FILDES
The Doctor

Carnation, Lily, Lily, Rose

MICHAEL HULSE

Of the several answers to darkness, better than sleep
and lovelier is the lighting of lanterns in gardens,
the claustrophiliac revelation of closeness, light
laden with intimate comfort: important harmony!
            Two girls in white

inhabit this acquiescent tenderness, Alices
cool in Marian shifts, innocents lavender-scented
and cotton-stockinged – you think of Betjeman's bicycle-
riding Oxford girls, the avuncular arousal these
            slim-limbed little

women trigger. What kind of Eden *is* this, anyway,
where only emblematic flowers grow? – carnations for the
experience of blood, lilies for virginity, and
roses modest and flushed (Lolitadom of girlhood!) like
            laundered bloodstained

linen. They are not girls but ideas of girls, and in
the otherworld of intimate green already their thoughts
are of leaving their paradise, as women in Watteau
dream of flying: see, it is in their serious faces
            taking the glow.

JOHN SINGER SARGENT
Carnation, Lily, Lily, Rose

Siesta

GARETH OWEN

Each day at this same hour
He comes to her
His lady of the afternoons.
Behind closed lids she hears the whispering brush strokes
Gathering in the light, the windows and her sleeping form.
Her countenance is often in his dreams
But these are things not spoken of.
Outside the room where all this happens
In a splash of sunlight by the kitchen door
A maid trades amorous gossip with the gardener's boy
While shelling peas into her widespread lap;
A petal falls, someone puts out washing
And in the orchard among oranges
Her husband, whose idea it was,
Tends to his bees, his face inside a net.
'I'm working on your mouth,' the painter tells her.
She does not know his christian name.
Her shut lids tremble. Just so
She used to close her eyes in childhood
Feigning sleep or death
Then open them in sudden laughter
To see her father's great moon face
Filling the everywhere;
Then later he was further off
And later still an absence
Like a place she took her heart to ache in.
Remembering this, she feels herself

Absorbed into the room
And in the darkness there
Beyond the limits of herself
Senses the painter with his canvas gone away
And lines of curious, reverential strangers
Filing past the open door
To gaze on her
Like one already dead.

JOHN FREDERICK LEWIS
The Siesta

Thank Heaven for Little Girls

SYLVIA KANTARIS

Six little girls in front like stained-glass
saints in stiff Pre-Raphaelite brocade
have lost their place already in the two-line text.
A budding Thomasina on the far left
entertains grave doubts about the words.
The youngest needs to be excused *in media res*.

You'd think the bigger girls in bulging smocks
would make a point of looking jubilant
but two (extreme left) find the text abhorrent.
I suspect the one who didn't even bother
to change out of her plain old burnt sienna
of chanting 'Rhubarb, rhubarb' *sotto voce*. Alleluia.

It's no wonder that the dark girl with the sad face
(right) seems confused about her function here –
posed for a Pietà, out of context –
unlike the elevated centrepiece,
ecstatic in the role of Christ. Her gender
gives a double edge of satire to the picture.

She is the only one of age who isn't pregnant yet,
though clothed in green and gold like Mother Earth
amongst these fidgety disciples who were not designed
to worship either gods or goddesses.
Alleluia therefore, and thank Heaven that most girls
make short shrift of apostolic attitudes.

THOMAS GOTCH
Alleluia

Rodin's Muse

ALISON FELL

She writhes like hawthorns,
is dark and demented,
her impossibly heavy head
a branch of thoughts the winds
have knotted. In all violence

she loans herself, (this muse
who promised him a flat blue
slate to shine his shadow on)
Her calves are rivers
from the glacial snout,

her bruised elbows abut
a space mute and compressing
as rock. The torture starts
not in the lovely torque
of the belly, or even gravity itself,

(this muse who gives no release,
is not delicate, does not dance)
but in a black burning at the pit
of the throat, a capture
of pain and angles somewhere
between his heart and her silence

AUGUSTE RODIN
The Muse

Rodin's 'The Kiss'

RUTH SILCOCK

I think that 'The Kiss' may be partly mine.
We all of us bought it, coming and going,
Our silver and copper gathered and growing
To flower into this.

I think I may own the dip in her spine,
Or his right thumb-nail, or her ankle-bone.
We could each claim our stake in this couple of stone –
Heel or knee, here it is.

We public have paid for these lovers, their crate
And insurance and travel and hoist through some door,
To settle, still kissing, on this piece of floor
Near postcards and coats.

We can sit on the circular seats and debate
The sculptor who found them, manhandled them out,
Caressing and tender, what true love's about,
His breath in their throats.

Models, wry-necked with a crick and a chill
From stretching and bending, embracing so long,
Have given their bodies to rock. They belong,
Petrified into bliss.

Petrified, silenced, separate, still,
The rag-bags of women, the cast skin and bone,
Whose life was sucked out and transformed into stone
Which we own, called 'The Kiss'.

AUGUSTE RODIN
The Kiss

73

The Bowl of Milk

JOHN LOVEDAY

In a moment the little black cat will be gone,
The bowl of milk set down somewhere
Outside the picture-space. Alone
Upstairs, Marthe will undress, prepare
The ritual water, soap herself, and lie,
Becoming innocent. The cat will drop
Asleep in the sun, the milk bowl dry.
Bonnard will paint sunlight on the table top.

PIERRE BONNARD
The Bowl of Milk

A Chair in my House: after Gwen John

JENNY JOSEPH

The house is very still and it is very quiet.
The chair stands in the hall: lines on the air;
Bar back, a plane of wood, focus in a space
Polished by dusk and people who might sit there.

Pieces of matter have made it. To get in words
What you could do in paint
Only the simplest sentences will serve.

And in this presence how much 'elsewhere' lurks.
It is a sort of listening to the air
That laps the object, a breathing in of light
That's needed if we are to see the chair.

Here I pare this little stick of words
To keep away the crowds
And set my chair down, which words can never do.

GWEN JOHN
A Lady Reading

The yellow daisies clash in the wind outside
It's not for long we can ignore they're there
Your noisy letters are dead in a box in the town
Your pictures breathe this wordless atmosphere.

The day goes through the room: dusk, white wall, through
To dusk again, and my wooden chair stands there.
I cannot get my chair the way you do
The things you paint.
Even the simplest sentence will not do.

Millbank

ELIZABETH BARTLETT

I think of the prisoners banged up
here, looking out over the Thames
from the dark side of the street.
As we climb the white steps together
and try to insert ourselves inside
one glass segment of the swing doors,
instead of two, I tread on dead faces
with my unsuitable clacking heels,
murdering the air with words.

We should have come with our eyes
held in our hands to meet the girl
holding a cat on her lap, who has,
after all, eluded us, leaving behind
an empty chair, a saucer of milk
on the floor, a note on the door.
There are cat hairs like brush strokes
all over my black jacket and bars
painted over all the windows.

We have been let out on parole
for a few hours. I have touched
her lover's statue and had my hand
cut off. You have come eye to eye
with Ezra Pound at last, and we have
picked all the erotic fruit greedily
from the cake without first concealing
a file in the middle. Outside, the wind
is as cold as an iron bracelet.

The Tate Gallery stands on the site of Millbank Penitentiary (1812–1892)

GWEN JOHN
Young Woman holding a Black Cat

The Merry-go-Round at Night

A variation of Rilke's 'Das Karussell'

DANNIE ABSE

The roof turns, the brassy merry-go-round crashes
    out music. Gaudy horses gallop tail to snout,
    inhabit the phantasmagoria of light
    substantial as smoke. Then each one vanishes.

Some pull carriages. Some children, frightened, hold tight
    the reins as they arrive and disappear
    chased by a scarlet lion that seems to sneer
    not snarl. And here's a unicorn painted white.

Look! From another world this strange, lit retinue.
    A boy on a steer, whooping, loud as dynamite –
    a sheriff, no doubt, though dressed in sailor-blue.
    And here comes the unicorn painted white.

Faster! The children spellbound, the animals prance,
    and this is happiness, this no-man's land
    where nothing's forbidden. And hardly a glance
    at parents who smile, who *think* they understand

    as the scarlet lion leaps into the night
    and here comes the unicorn painted white.

AUTHOR'S NOTE PAGE 153

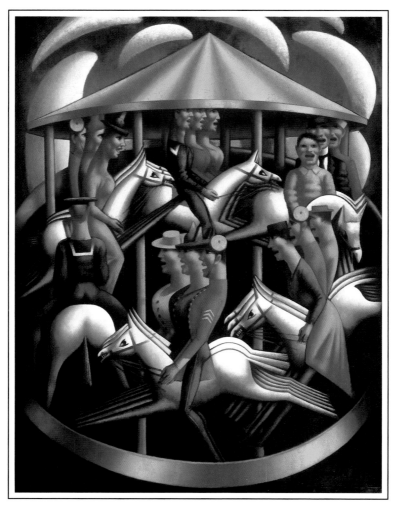

MARK GERTLER
The Merry-go-Round

A Place

EMILY MITCHELL

I remember it well,
A grove of oaks with a stream
And a fence, which had fallen in places
But still stood in others
I remember
How calm and quiet and green it was
And how the stream, bubbling along,
was the only sound breaking the stillness
And I remember
The sun light falling on the field beyond the grove
And a calf, venturing from its mothers side,
stopping to drink at the stream
Before returning to the rest of the herd
And how that place,
So quiet and peaceful,
Awakened my mind
From a deep sleep

SPENCER GORE
Letchworth

Edvard Munch: 'The Sick Child'

JEREMY HOOKER

'Disease, insanity and death were the angels
which attended my cradle.' – Edvard Munch

North is a dark green sea;
the boy shaking on the bed
was born to it – he is wrack

opening and shutting in the tide;
a ribbed shell dragged down,
which waves knock
and the brine swills;

a mariner who will not drown.

Angels attend him
far into the cold:

a woman the sea has broken on,
bowing her down;
a girl with red hair, face
fragile as a moon
that floats out on the dark.

AUTHOR'S NOTE PAGE 158

EDVARD MUNCH
The Sick Child

The Miracle of
the Bottle and the Fishes

CHARLES TOMLINSON

I

What is it Braque
would have us see in this
piled-up table-top of his?

One might even take it for
a cliff-side, sky-high
accumulation opening door on door

of space. We do not know
with precision or at a glance
which is space and which is substance,

nor should we yet: the eye must stitch
each half-seen, separate
identity together

in a mind delighted and disordered by
a freshness of the world's own weather.

To enter space anew:
to enter a new space
inch by inch and not
the perspective avenue

GEORGES BRAQUE
Bottle and Fishes

cutting a swathe through mastered distance
from a viewpoint that is single:
'If you painted nothing but profiles
you would grow to believe
men have only one eye.'
Touch must supply
space with its substance and become
a material of the exploration
as palpable as paint,
in a reciprocation where
things no longer stand
bounded by emptiness: 'I begin,'
he says, 'with the background
that supports the picture
like the foundation of a house.'

III

These layered darknesses
project no image of a mind
in collusion with its spectres:
in this debate
of shadow and illumination fate
does not hang heavily
over an uncertain year
(it is nineteen-twelve) for the eye
leaves fate undone
refusing to travel straitened
by either mood or taken measure:
it must stumble, it must touch
to guess how much of space
for all its wilderness
is both honeycomb and home.

The Green Mare's Advice to the Cows

GEORGE SZIRTES

'It seemed that the cow was conducting
world politics at that time' – Marc Chagall

I

What matters is the price of the mare.
What matters is the colour of the street.
What matters is that streets have no colour to speak of
Until we give them colours. The same with names.
What matters is the sound of arguments
And not their content. Arguments are blue,
Which, incidentally, is the colour of the street
(And hence, you see, I show them arguing.)
What matters is the Love of God
And never mind if God does not exist.
You make him yellow, just as Christ is white,
But that damn cockerel keeps getting in,
And cows with their seductive eyes and udders,
And violinists who can only scrape.
It is another music altogether
That we dance to – and it isn't much
But it will do, believe me, it will do.

2

Surrender to mere *brio?* Stiff
Heads float off in disbelief
And fingers multiply in grief.

A clock strikes midnight in the air
In homage to Apollinaire.
Let Malevich adore the square.

Those who are less innocent
Castrate, carve up, dissect, invent
With a much sharper instrument.

A brush is fine. In mute arrest
A country bumpkin cups the breast
Of tender Vacha. Cows are best.

Cows will run the government.
Cows have a delightful scent.
Cows produce their Testament.

You watch the carnival proceed
Down muddy streets. The cows will lead
The moujiks home while altars bleed

With gentle bovine sacrifice,
Both melancholy and precise.
You cannot kill the same cow twice.

You see the calf, you see the child
Within the womb: Vitebsk, a wild
Impatience, dirty, undefiled.

MARC CHAGALL
The Green Mare

The commissars may rave and row
The housepainters obey you now
And hang the banner of the Cow.

The frozen cow hangs like a star,
And you yourself a commissar –
You start to moo. Yes, you'll go far.

Remember Grandfather, who stood
Before you with his feet in blood:
'Now look here, cow, we must have food.'

First grub, then dreams. But Lenin stands
All topsy-turvy on his hands.
What sacrifice the state demands.

The cows will take you at your word,
Advancing on you in a herd.
One cow takes wing, soars like a bird.

But look up there. The dream clouds fly
Above nightmare artillery
And cows are raining from the sky,

Dead cows, contented cows. It pays
To trust their unaffected ways
And leave their ghosts a land to graze.

   3
The Man who is a Cello and the Fish who plays
The Violin are suddenly struck dumb.

The Goat in the Sky grows horns of logic. He weighs
Too much and every puzzle and conundrum
Begins to feel the lack of a solution.
The puritans claim back their revolution.

The poet, no longer cut in pieces, does not lie
Flat on the grass in the formal posture of death.
The egotistic lovers neither kiss nor fly.
The riddled milkmaid sinks down out of breath.
The dead man's candles cannot light the street
And broken bodies rest on tired feet.

The village processions reverse their steps. They realise
The city they inhabit has always been there, waiting.
The samovar slips off the crooked table. The eyes
Of the dead calf are finally shut. The dating
Couples are dated. The pendulum is still
And time runs down like water from the hill.

4

Returning to the green mare. She is grinning
At the wild commotion. All those words and colours
Merely confirm her own view of aesthetics:
No artist ever paints quite what he sees.
No artist ever tries to paint his dreams.
An artist only paints what he believes in.
And she is winking, full of self-belief
And green intestines, though she knows the town
Is changing irredeemably behind her.
She tells the cows: your freedom is exciting.
She tells the cows: prepare for government.

Paul Klee: 'They're Biting'

PAUL MULDOON

The lake supports some kind of bathysphere,
an Arab dhow

and a fishing-boat
complete with languorous net.

Two anglers
have fallen hook, line and sinker

for the goitred,
spiny fish-caricatures

with which the lake is stocked.
At any moment all this should connect.

When you sent me a postcard of *They're Biting*
there was a plane sky-writing

I LOVE YOU over Hyde Park.
Then I noticed the exclamation-mark

at the painting's heart.
It was as if I had already heard

a waist-thick conger
mouthing NO from the fishmonger's

otherwise-drab window
into which I might glance to check my hair.

PAUL KLEE
They're Biting (Sie beissen an)

97

The Uncertainty of the Poet

WENDY COPE

I am a poet.
I am very fond of bananas.

I am bananas.
I am very fond of a poet.

I am a poet of bananas.
I am very fond,

A fond poet of 'I am, I am' –
Very bananas,

Fond of 'Am I bananas?
Am I?' – a very poet.

Bananas of a poet!
Am I fond? Am I very?

Poet bananas! I am.
I am fond of a 'very'.

I am of very fond bananas.
Am I a poet?

GIORGIO DE CHIRICO
The Uncertainty of the Poet

Telephone to Nowhere

SARAH JANE RATHERHAM

'Danger!' cries the voice, 'Danger!'
Danger screaming in every thread of the line,
But the vigilant watchers have long since crept away;
They do not hear the anguish as every word is spoken –
The words are lost in the spray.

In the loneliest place in the world, no-one can hear you cry.

Shuddering, the words catch the wind, and split the night
in two,
Shattering the deep well of silence and pouring the darkness in,
Flinging the sleeping water up in a cloud of silver stars;
But echoing from brow-beaten rocks, the cry rides back
Unanswered.

It's the loneliest place in the world, where no-one can
hear you cry.

'Danger!' screams the voice, 'Danger!'
It is felt in every inch of crackling line –
'Someone needs your help, some ship has lost its battle' –
But the snails drag slowly over it, no-one heeds
And no-one hears.

In the loneliest place in the world, there's no-one left to
hear.

SALVADOR DALI
Mountain Lake

The Lobster on the Telephone

ELEANOR SNOW

I saw a lobster
Yellowish and orangish
Sitting on a telephone.
And I said
'Does your mummy know you are here
You naughty lobster?
Did she say yes?'
The lobster curled his legs
Tiredly and crossly.

SALVADOR DALI
Lobster Telephone

Henry Moore: 'Woman Seated in the Underground'

GEORGE MACKAY BROWN

How many thousands of years she has travelled
To come to this place.

Above, burning wind
Broken stone and water.

She has sat in Troy and Carthage and Warsaw.
She has endured ice and sun.
She sits, pure from those weatherings.

Is she waiting for the hunters and soldiers to come home?

Does she hear
The laughter of lost children?

She breaks the long vigil
With spinning, baking, gossip, welcomes and farewells. In April
   she will set daffodils in a jar.

Fires, shaking of cornerstones!
Nineteen-forty. This is her longest winter.

London is burning and breaking above her.
Persephone, wait on your throne.

HENRY MOORE
Woman Seated in the Underground

'Woman Seated in the Underground', 1941

CAROL ANN DUFFY

I forget. I have looked at the other faces and found
no memory, no love. *Christ, she's a rum one.*
Their laughter fills the tunnel, but it does not
comfort me. There was a bang and then
I was running with the rest through smoke. Thick, grey
smoke has covered thirty years at least.
I know I am pregnant, but I do not know my name.

Now they are singing. *Underneath the lantern*
by the barrack gate. But waiting for whom?
Did I? I have no wedding ring, no handbag, nothing.
I want a fag. I have either lost my ring or I am
a loose woman. No. Someone has loved me. Someone
is looking for me even now. I live somewhere.
I sing the word *darling* and it yields nothing.

Nothing. A child is crying. Mine doesn't show yet.
Baby. My hands mime the memory of knitting.
Purl. Plain. I know how to do these things, yet my mind
has unravelled into thin threads that lead nowhere.
In a moment, I shall stand up and scream until
somebody helps me. The skies were filled with sirens, planes,
fire, bombs, and I lost myself in the crowd. Dear God.

HENRY MOORE, *Seated Figure*, 1970–1
photograph: courtesy of the
Henry Moore Foundation

Entrance to a Lane

DAVID GASCOYNE

to Elizabeth Jennings

Memento rectangled to lead the gaze
From outer levels to a hub of white,
An elsewhere that recedes from coiling planes

Sequestered rural scene reputed Welsh,
Season's regalia reduced to tones
Of veld and verdure, leaves to sprays of blotch

A static vortex wherein ochre glows
Softly in strata linked by streaks and zones
Of compact shade and layers of virid light

The felt-floored lane leads to a blank where hues
And perceptions vanish as fast as time
Into the *non-lieu* beyond mortal reach

Where red is not an opposite of rot
Or devastation the reverse of peace
And all those things that were the case resume.

GRAHAM SUTHERLAND
Entrance to a Lane

Summer: Young September's Corn Field

JEREMY REED

A sky of brilliant ultramarine
stands off without imprinting a shadow
on the blond sibilance of dusted corn.
Whichever way the wind moves there's a flow –

a current set up in responsive ears.
Today it's calm. September, the earth's crust
is parched, blood-spots of scarlet pimpernel
and red poppies are filmed with a thin dust,

the landscape is unpeopled, leave a field
and it defines its own contours, no edge
serves as a clear boundary, things overtake
their limits, bindweed stitches up a hedge . . .

Dead silence here. They're listening for rain
in the farm out of the picture grouped round
a wooden table, a bluebottle drums
in a net curtain. It's the only sound.

ALAN REYNOLDS
Summer: Young September's Cornfield

Stand in the foreground, shapes are menacing,
too huge, too close-up, look, the holly-green
corn-ears are feathery vertical spears.
They threaten as a colony that's seen

only by the eye looking out across
the landscape, trees retreating up a hill,
and perhaps invisibly a farmhand
prostrate in the centre, so very still

he doesn't move for the wasp on his face;
the dead bottles are skittled round his feet.
But something's waiting. It's the border state
of growth that's untouched by the grizzled heat,

or machinery preparing to roll?
Tomorrow harvesters will work the field,
mangle the farmhand, equalize the corn.
The beetle runs beneath its cobalt shield.

The Arrest – on Seeing Matisse's Painting 'The Snail'

JAMES BERRY

Green has a place like the heart.
More shapes of colours take
attention, at the centre.
They look hung out like washing
of mostly handkerchiefs
in motion, going circular.

Underneath, a patch of white
is papered on like sky
on a base of sun-earth. Then
this level offers other happened
shapes, like apertures or windows –
all views you would have
if flying, or crawling
or walking or standing still.

Now the colours are pools
of emotions – tones
that make an alphabet of moods.
They could be musical sounds
that left bodies of tones
and shapes in a precise order
but appear spontaneous.

HENRI MATISSE
The Snail

You are toned up.
Sources are exposed here,
arranged, in these pieces
of colours, these offsprings
of the sun, that have
their family difference richness.

An expanse of blue is meditative.
Strangely, an earthy-red becomes
a field like a vast bed.
You sense renewal
in a mask of sleep.
An awareness of purple robes
passes, like a breath-wave of wind.

The picture is a language.
It will not yield up everything.
You question yourself about
an interpretation of a coiled
movement. And, really, how
does snail-shell appropriate
such a range of tone?

You walk away. You wake up
in a warm rain. You see
that milked from sunlight
the pieces of colours are segments
hanging out a vision – a life's
circle that crept, into a spiral.

The Rothko Room

GILLIAN CLARKE

He crushed charcoal with a city's rubies,
saw such visions of soft-edged night and day
as stop the ears with silence. In this,
the last room after hours in the gallery,
a mesh diffuses London's light and sound.
The Indian keeper nods to sleep, marooned
in a trapezium of black on red.

We few who stop are quiet as if we prayed
in this room after Turner's turbulence.
Coming and going through paint's water-curtains
turning a corner suddenly we find
a city burns, a cathedral comes down
with a last blaze filling its gaudy lantern
and windows buckle as a tenement falls.

Rack the heart for memory or sense
and reds like these come crowding out of dream:
musk mallow, goat's rue, impatiens,
loosestrife, hellebore, belladonna, nightshade,
poppysilks crushed in their velvety soot,
and digitalis purpurea, red on maroon,
drop dappled gloves along an August lane.

A morning's laundry marking glass with steam
on rainy Mondays where a blackbird sings
sodden in dripping dark-red lilac trees.
We look, myopic, down his corridors
through misted spectacles of broken glass
window on window, scaffolding of pain
red on maroon and black, black on maroon.

THE ROTHKO ROOM

Into the Rothko Installation

PETER REDGROVE

Dipping into the Tate
As with the bucket of oneself into a well
Of colour and odour, to smell the pictures
And the people steaming in front of the pictures,
To sniff up the odours of the colours, which are
The fragrances of people excited by the pictures;
As the pair walk down the gallery
On each side of them the Turners glow
As though they both were carrying radiance
In a lantern whose rays filled the hall like wings
That brushed the images, which glowed;

Into the Installation, which smells
Of lacquered canvas soaking up all fragrance,
Of cold stone, and her scent falters
Like cloth torn in front of the Rothkos
Which are the after-images of a door slammed
So blinding-white the artist must shut his eyes
And paint the colours floating in his darkness.

He chose the darkest of the images for that white,
That green; red on red beating to the point
Where the eye gasps, and gives up its perfume
Like a night-flowering plant; and with many
Thin washes he achieves the effect
Of a hidden light source which smells
Like water far off in the night, the eye
So parched; paintings you almost can't see;

As if in painting
The Israelites crossing the Red Sea
He painted the whole wall red, and,
Black on black therein,
God somewhat like a lintel. We brought
The lanterns of ourselves in here
And your imagination blotted our light up, Rothko;
The black reached out, quenching our perfume
As in a dark chapel, dark with torn pall,
And our eyes were lead, sinking
Into that darkness all humans have for company;

Standing there, eyes wide, her lids faltered
And closed, and 'I see it, now' she said
And in her breath a wonderful blaze
Of colour of her self-smell
Where she saw that spirit-brightness
Of a door slammed open, and a certain green insertion
Shifting as her gaze searched
What seemed like a meadow through the white door
Made of lightning, cloud or flowers, like Venusberg
Opening white portals in the green mountain
Stuffed with light, he having used
The darkest of all that spectrum almost to blindness

And in his studio in the thin chalk of dawn
Having passed inwardly through that blackness,
Slitting his wrists, by process of red on red
He entered the chapel under the haunted mound
Where the white lightning of another world
Flashed, and built pillars. We left
The gallery of pictures rocked
By the perfume of slammed eye, its corridors
Were wreathed with the detonation of all its pictures
In the quick of the eye, delighting into
Perfumes like fresh halls of crowded festival.

A Painter Painted

MICHAEL HAMBURGER

Portrait or nature morte or landscape (nature vivante) –
Pencil and brush make all a still life, fixed,
So that the wind that swept, breath that came hard
Or easy, when wind has dropped, breath has passed on,
The never visible, may stir again in stillness.

Visible both, the painter and the painted
Passed by me, four decades ago. We met,
We talked, we drank, and we went our ways.
This head's more true than the head I saw.
Closed, these lips tell me more than the lips that spoke.
Lowered, these eyes are better at looking.

A likeness caught? No. Pictor invenit.
Slowly, slowly, under his lowered eyelids
He worked, against time, to find the face grown truer,
Coax it to life in paint's dead millimetres,
Compose them into nature, in a light
That is not London's, any hour's or year's;

Furrow it, too, with darkness; let in the winds
That left their roads, painter's and painted's, littered,
Brought branches down, scattering feathers, fruit,
Though for a moment only, stopped the bland flow of breath.

And here it hangs, the still life of a head.

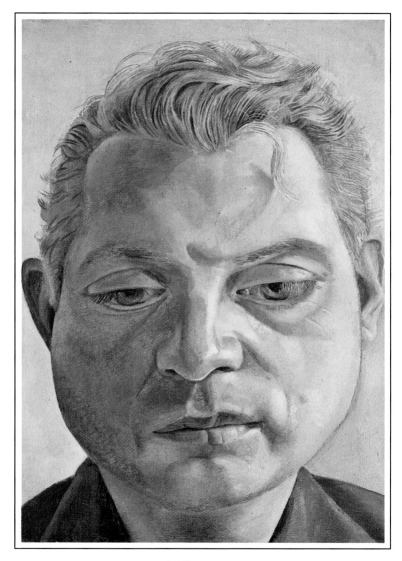

LUCIEN FREUD
Portrait of Francis Bacon

Poems after Francis Bacon

ANNE STEVENSON

personality, the flesh artist
(and presiding self-portrait)
has perfected his trick of exposing
bodies to money
until they attain metallic
putrefaction.

when these hunks of human stuff
harden into fixed forms
reptilian man thinks in one circle,
mammalian woman in another.

her gold ring is larger and brighter
than his rink of empire.

that fury in a cage
is their offspring.

she has sprung fully armed
from their heads,
and she means to hate them.

at present she's
spooling her childhood
in her chittering skull.

AUTHOR'S NOTE PAGE 163

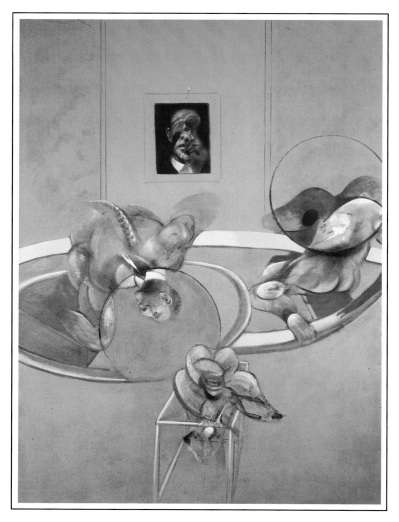

FRANCIS BACON
Three Figures and Portrait

Poems after Francis Bacon

ANNE STEVENSON

self-placed,
for years he's struggled to achieve it,
a position exactly at the centre
of his invisible frame.

the red carpet and expensive kirman
congratulate his shoes.
the rich blue furniture, discreet blue curtain,
push forward his expression of
resourceful authority, a farsighted
gaze to the future, though
tensely he holds in readiness
shortsighted spectacles – for details.

you can put your faith in me,
says the strong right shoulder,
but the left will not bear
the weight of responsibility;
he's had to remove it
to centre the picture on
righteousness.

shift him three inches to the left
and everything's lost.

AUTHOR'S NOTE PAGE 163

FRANCIS BACON
Seated Figure

Teeth

BLAKE MORRISON

And here – come closer – framed so you can
See yourself in it, my Francis Bacon.
Early, yes, but far from an apprentice piece
So the experts reassure me. Those sharp eyes
And the gaoling of the figure in a boxroom
Are as typical of Bacon as the scream.
A Pope, the title says, but it's left open
To be read as anyone in pain –
A car-ace, say, burning in his Jaguar
Or a murderer in a high electric chair.
But look, don't let me preach. Just take a pew
And relax – whisky all right for you?

Yes, worth a fortune now, but back then
In the forties, when he showed at the Redfern,
Bacon was the coming man. There was this chap
From the Gallery got one for me cheap,
No questions asked. But then Janine, my first wife,
Wouldn't give it house-room for her life.
Dear God, you'd not believe the tongue she had:
What's that when it's at home, a gibbon head?

Piss off and get our money back at once.
I'll not surround myself with skeletons.
I tried to exchange the thing but couldn't:
We fought like cats until her accident
When she lost her head over some diplomat
And sat there, smashed, on a crossing in the mouth
Of the Glasgow express. I sent Hammond
To identify the bits . . . but never mind.

Andrea now – you met her coming up –
She's got her head screwed on. After a decent gap
She took the picture out of storage
And gave it pride of place. It takes some courage,
Eh, not liking it herself but knowing
The pleasure her husband gets from showing
It to business friends, who come to stare
Over a large Courvoisier and cigar.
The womanly virtues! Learning to cater
For a chap's *joie de vivre* and *raison d'être*.
Oh yes, my Andrea knows a trick or two –
Watch out or she'll be playing them on you.

Same again? What's that, his later stuff? Well,
It looks to me much as before: offal
On a mattress, paralysed limbs, the green eyes
Of people who're crazy with loneliness.
Not quite my thing, between ourselves: I rather hate
How his paintings constantly exaggerate.
One has one's setbacks but where's the point
In committing one's gloominess to paint.
Oh, I'd be off my head to let go of it
But were it choice not investment Dubuffet
Might be hanging here instead, an artist
Whose disfigurings are much more to my taste.

But look, you're not here for a seminar.
Empires have fallen, whole industries come near
To collapse – and all while we've been talking.
Outside the door my rivals are skulking
With a vengeance: I'll see their blood pizzle out
Sooner than be mastered, I'll wipe the lot.
So let's down to business in my study.
But notice, as you pass, how the steady
Eyes of that Pope seem to accuse and track
Us, as if we'd personally stretched him on that rack.
Just an artist's trick, friend – no need to get
Jumpy. We'll see that bastard roasting yet.

Five Morsels in the Form of Pears

EDWARD LUCIE-SMITH

for William Scott and Erik Satie

I

Personal problem: how to
get over that wall and sink
my teeth into a beauty?
The orchard is a harem –
swelling hips and large bottoms.
You can almost hear them, those
female conversations
about their jewels and children,
about their seeds and raindrops,
new life and how to make it.

2

That black-and-yellow buzzing –
a nest of guards to punish
the intruder. Swollen with
stings, you'll regret your boldness.
Ah! the pain of the half-shut
wounded eye that looked too close
at imprisoned love! It is
not like that. Every wasp
is choosing a bride, palping
flesh and savouring juices.

3

They are courting their tethered
victims, who hang by a stem
between air and earth, between
growing and dying. The wasps
walk on the surprisingly
chapped skin, and then probe and probe.
You expect a convulsive
movement, a tiny outcry
as virginity is lost
while the wound opens, oozes.

4

How swift the transition
from favourite to mother!
You would not care, now, for what
this broadhipped woman offers:
a family of grubs in
an impassive form which has
passed in a moment from ripe
to rotten. You did not come
in time. 'It is all over,'
she says, meaning her sweetness.

5

In another part of the
orchard, and hanging from a
different tree; or perhaps
on a plate on a table,
squatting there half-tilted and
content to wait. It arrives,

the moment of decision.
They know they are fortunate
to be thus summoned, looked at,
picked for the preservative
violations of art.

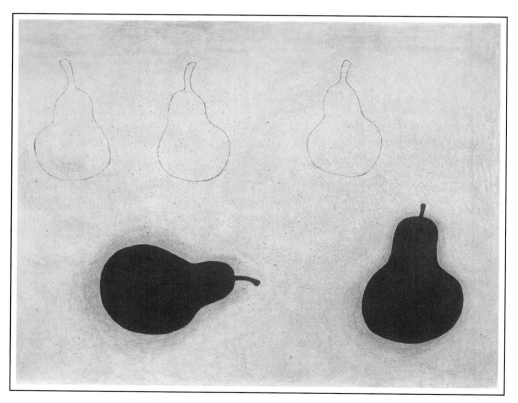

WILLIAM SCOTT
Pears

Oi yoi yoi

VICKI FEAVER

to Roger Hilton about his painting in the Tate

The lady has no shame.
Wearing not a stitch
she is lolloping across
an abstract beach
towards a notional sea.

I like the whisker
of hair under her armpit.
It suggests that she's not
one of those women who's always
trying to get rid of their smell.

You were more interested
in her swinging baroque tits
and the space between her thighs
than the expression on her face.
That you've left blank.

But her mons venus
you've etched in black ink
with the exhuberance of a young lad
caught short on a bellyfull of beer
scrawling on the wall in the Gents.

As a woman I ought to object.
But she looks happy enough.
And which of us doesn't occasionally
want one ot the Old Gods to come down
and chase us over the sands.

ROGER HILTON
Oi yoi yoi

Awakening

RICHARD BURNS

*Sur la pente du talus, les anges tournent leurs robes de
laine dans les herbages d'acier et d'émeraude.* – Rimbaud

A scent of female angels in this dawn
Beckons me, half asleep, to mount their hill
Whose green gilt daggers, pointed up at heaven,
Accuse my burning nights of birth in hell.
Ah, but I've escaped now, safe with these wool-robed creatures.
    They flee from me who sometime did me seek
    For flame, I cannot move or think or speak.

Fire rises on my right from dream-torn battles,
But, look, how dawn progresses on my left.
My woolly angels bleat. Like whorled sea-conches
They moan and murmur, hurrying me aloft
Out of reach of my feverish nightmare murderers.
    They mingle breeze, warmth, thyme and lanolin,
    With vision, they leap into brain and skin.

Below, around, float soft abysmal stars,
Pouring, as from a basket, overflowing,
Invisible, as flakes of summer sunlight
Or angels, now it is morning, petals flying,
As, down from my drowsy hill, I slide into daybreak.
    Abysmal angels, sacrificial sheep,
    Protect me, I have woken from my sleep.

AUTHOR'S NOTE PAGE 155

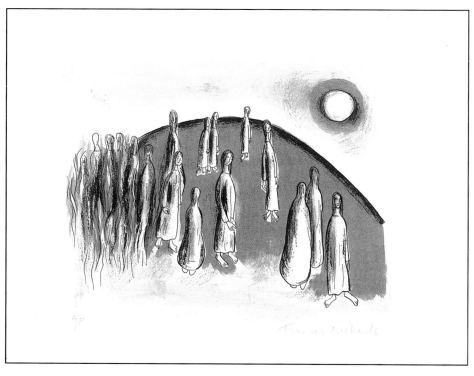

FRANCES RICHARDS
Les Illuminations

The Bench

EDWIN MORGAN

Honey-brown varnish glistens: Easter hymn.
Even its WET PAINT sign sings out spring's here.
It's sturdy, foursquare, brown, abstract, and clear.
Nothing could make the backdrop tree buds dim
or undo wonder from the sharp fresh green
of daffodil strikes but this silent thing
that sits and shouts, a throne to kid a king,
and when he rises, nakedness is seen.
But nothing sticks except a twig, dropped there
by frenziedly building crows. The March wind
tugs at it, but it will not stir, or mar
perfection less by letting the air bare
its print. No caws, no nest, no brood is thinned.
The first to brush the twig off sees the scar.

One thing is certain, it is not abstract.
Who can see the wooden slats for five, six
people, a dog (seven!), pigeons, a mix
of life as warm in its midsummer fact
and midday pause as ever hit a park
with one moment withdrawn from every pain?
Crackle of crisps lost in hot blue space, brain
at a drowsy crossword, crumbs in an ark
of fingers held out (holy that too!) as
treasures for motley wings and scavengers,

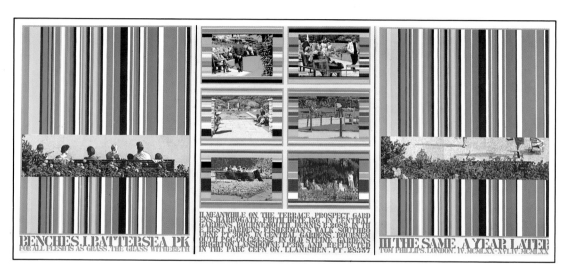

TOM PHILLIPS
Benches

mingled with 'I don't know, that's what he said –'
and '– wants one of those instant cameras'
and '– nice bit of ham –'; those passengers
race in their happiness towards the dead.

Leaves die, but not the tree, not yet, not soon.
Red, yellow, crinkled, papery, they scrape
along the bench, collect at the slumped shape
of a tramp; they've nothing to say; forenoon,
afternoon he sleeps, stirs, shifts, mutters, feels
October probing sluggish arteries,
clutches his coat like a cloak. Batteries
of sleet wait to be loosed, not yet. With squeals
cut by rising gusts, children chase and dart.
There is a thud of chestnuts, and one breaks.
What a soft sheeny tender eye looks out
in wonder from its shattered shell! Take heart
it says. The old man stares at it. The rakes
rattle in sheds, there is a far-off shout –

never heard in the whiteness over all
and the seat quite filled with high-drifted snow
like a dust-sheeted hurdy-gurdy. Go
by it still, good winter walkers! The fall
of silent feet dislodges a few grains.
Whistle and breath might melt a dozen more.
But suddenly all flakes are in uproar:
a great floundering setter coughs and strains
and leaves his lead, flounces onto the bench
through wet white flying sprays and veils, and skids
wild claws along the wood at last, shakes, barks,
a snowdog breaking bonds, his boisterous wrench
shows sage winter callow. With white eyelids
he grins; his master laughs. They see lambs, larks.

Percy

DAVID RODGER

The century wrote its will
but the century did not die.
Impoverished heirs still
– the tropical butterfly,

the Great Barrier Reef –
waited for salvation
(first the explosion of grief
and then regeneration).

The century painted its prayers
on canvas and cut them in stone
– not for it religious airs
or the Gregorian drone.

It stored its prayers away
like ammonites in the rock,
it appointed priests to display
its amulets to the flock

and it begged that there might be mercy
in future aeons of dark
for white-furred *Percy*
and *Mr and Mrs Clark.*

DAVID HOCKNEY
Mr and Mrs Clark and Percy

But futile were its vaults.
After the day of ire
remained only basalts
crystallised in the fire.

Pray for the next régime:
no privet and polyanthus;
osmunda growing supreme,
no laurel or acanthus.

Butterflies and epiphytes,
polyps and sea-slugs,
no tours of city sights,
no commemorative mugs.

Percy prowling the wild;
willow herb in the room
where Percy posed as the child
of parents musing in gloom.

The Badminton Game

CONNIE BENSLEY

That morning, I awoke and went down
just as I was, in my green slippers
to look at the hydrangea mariesii –
the only flower Clifton allows in the garden,
for he must have his trees and shrubs.

Out I crept, my slippers darkening in the dew,
and hearing a movement behind me
I turned and found Ruth. She was carrying
the racquets; and so – smiling, not speaking –
we ran between the great bushes to the net,

and there we played (quietly, of course,
so that Uncle Edward might not hear)
until the breakfast gong recalled us.
We ran up the back stairs en deshabille,
and down the front ones, decorous but tardy,

and kissed Uncle Edward; but I took care
to embrace him as he likes best, to forestall
reproof. Colour rose up behind his moustache
and his face worked silently, but then he vanished,
as usual, behind *The Times*.

DAVID INSHAW
The Badminton Game

Lines for Richard Long

JOHN JAMES

the grey colour of a pear
in the quiet light of the kitchen
the glittering branches at the window

the force of the hearth breaks out
invoking name & lineage

it's a good step
that will continue to the end without arriving

When you take up your pack & go
to the remote & desert places of the Earth
your path is a watercourse
or a torrent on the slope

the walker in summer-time on slanting ground
in a robe of vapour

by night there will be shelter
in the hollow & the cleft

I was a walker in earth before I was proficient in learning
catching the deep night & dawn divide
the line of the curling wave on the extended shore

now the leg thinks in distance & the arm in weights

CLOUD SUN CLOUD THUNDER CLOUD HAIL RAIN SUN

Saturday lime Sunday oak & quick-thorn
the place of the little drop & the length of the Avon
when it fills when it overflows
when it disappears in a dark thicket
quick sunlight between clouds

& from above the tops of the whirling trees
measure the veil of the drops in the air
at the width of the river's mouth
when the sea is turning round

the words in the book & the book in its beginning

AUTHOR'S NOTE PAGE 159

RICHARD LONG
Slate Circle

Swinging Men

DAVID FROMMER

I was waiting in the rotunda
When I spotted an anaconda
Above my head
Behind a patch of red
Dancing on the ceiling
Were nine people

BRUCE MCLEAN
Construction of the Grey Flag

BRUCE MCLEAN
Study for Construction of the Grey Flag

Leaving the Tate

FLEUR ADCOCK

Coming out with your clutch of postcards
in a Tate Gallery bag and another clutch
of images packed into your head you pause
on the steps to look across the river

and there's a new one: light bright buildings,
a streak of brown water, and such a sky
you wonder who painted it – Constable? No:
too brilliant. Crome? No: too ecstatic –

a madly pure Pre-Raphaelite sky,
perhaps, sheer blue apart from the white plumes
rushing up it (today, that is,
April. Another day would be different

but it wouldn't matter. All skies work.)
Cut to the lower right for a detail:
seagulls pecking on mud, below
two office blocks and a Georgian terrace.

Now swing to the left, and take in plane-trees
bobbled with seeds, and that brick building,
and a red bus . . . Cut it off just there,
by the lamp-post. Leave the scaffolding in.

That's your next one. Curious how
these outdoor pictures didn't exist
before you'd looked at the indoor pictures,
the ones on the walls. But here they are now,

marching out of their panorama
and queuing up for the viewfinder
your eye's become. You can isolate them
by holding your optic muscles still.

You can zoom in on figure studies
(that boy with the rucksack), or still lives,
abstracts, townscapes. No one made them.
The light painted them. You're in charge

of the hanging committee. Put what space
you like around the ones you fix on,
and gloat. Art multiplies itself.
Art's whatever you choose to frame.

Biographical Index of Poets

DANNIE ABSE's *Collected Poems 1948–1976* was published by Hutchinson in 1977. A new volume of poems, *Ask the Bloody Horse*, has just been published by Century Hutchinson, and is a Poetry Book Society choice for the summer 1986. At present, with his wife Joan, he is editing *Voices in the Gallery*, a further anthology of poems and paintings which the Tate will publish in 1986.   [page 82]

Note: I was about to leave the Tate Gallery when Mark Gertler's painting 'Merry-Go-Round' made me hesitate. It intrigued me: the background of night, the tense, open-mouthed wooden figures in the artificial light whose enjoyment, if it were such, was akin to that of spectators at a horror film. Gertler painted it in 1916 and no doubt was making some allegorical statement about the First World War.

On the way home I kept thinking of Gertler's painting, its ambiguity, the terror in it, and then I recalled Rilke's poem about a Merry-Go-Round at night. How typical, I thought, of Rilke to focus on such an image, interested as he was in the mediation of the invisible into the visible. ('The Angel of the Duino Elegies,' he wrote, 'is the being who vouches for the recognition of a higher degree of reality in the invisible, terrible to us because we . . . still cling to the visible.') Yes, the Merry-Go-Round at night was a given metaphor for Rilke: fairground spectators have the optical illusion of night's invisible creatures becoming tangible as the roundabout turns them from darkness into light.

It was years since I had read Rilke's poem. When I arrived home I picked out Rilke's poems from the bookshelf. I read J.B. Leishman's translation of Das Karussell (I have no German, alas) and was astonished to discover I had misremembered the poem, that the Merry-Go-Round Rilke portrayed was not even one revolving at night! Somehow I must have merged Gertler's vision with my own weak remembrance of Rilke's poem. Doodling, I sat down to write the translation I thought I had remembered.

FLEUR ADCOCK was born in New Zealand in 1934 but has lived in England since 1963. Her latest publications are *Selected Poems* (Oxford University Press, 1983) and *The Virgin and the Nightingale* (translations of medieval Latin poems: Bloodaxe Books, 1963); she has also edited *The Oxford Book of Contemporary New Zealand Poetry* and a forthcoming Faber anthology of women's poetry.   [page 150]

COLIN ARCHER is a Social Services administrator in London. He started writing poetry in 1981, and his work has appeared in such magazines as *Outposts*, the *Literary Review*, *Iron*, *Other Poetry*, *Punch*, and *Poetry Nottingham*. [page 34]

ELIZABETH BARTLETT, who was born near Deal in Kent, left school at fifteen to work in a factory. A doctor's secretary for many years, she is now a free-lance writer, married, and living in Sussex. She has published three collections of verse, *A Lifetime of Dying* (1979), *Strange Territory* (1983), both published by Peterloo Poets, and more recently *The Czar is Dead*. In 1985 she was awarded an Arts Council bursary. [page 79]

PATRICIA BEER was born in Devon and educated at Exmouth Grammar School, Exeter University and St Hugh's College, Oxford. After teaching at the University of Padua and London University, she became a fulltime writer. She has published seven volumes of poetry, the most recent being *The Lie of the Land* (Hutchinson), an autobiography, a novel and two works of criticism. She is married to Damien Parsons; they live in Devon. [page 44]

CONNIE BENSLEY lives in South West London. She has had two collections of poetry published, *Progress Report* and *Moving In*, both by Harry Chambers/Peterloo Poets, and has had two short plays for radio broadcast. [page 144]

JAMES BERRY was born in a Jamaican village but has lived in Britain for most of his adult life. He has won prizes for both poetry and his prose writing. Recent publications include an anthology *News for Babylon* (Chatto & Windus) and *Chain of Days* (Oxford University Press). [page 113]

ALAN BROWNJOHN's *Collected Poems* was published in 1983, and his version of Goethe's *Torquato Tasso* in 1985. A new volume of poems is planned for 1986. He is currently Chairman of the National Poetry Centre (the Poetry Society.) [page 58]

RICHARD BURNS was born in London in 1943. His books include *Avebury, Some poems Illuminated by Frances Richards, Learning to Talk, Tree, Keys to Transformation, Roots/Routes*, and *Black Light*. He founded the Cambridge Poetry Festival.   [page 136]

Note: The poem included is part of a sequence written in memory of Frances Richards, who died last year, aged 84, and is based on her lithographs for Rimbaud's *Les Illuminations* (1975).

CHARLES CAUSLEY was born in Launceston, Cornwall. In 1967 he was awarded the Queen's Gold Medal for Poetry; he is also a Fellow of the Royal Society of Literature. The University of Exeter conferred on him the Honorary Degree of Doctor of Letters in 1977. His most recent books of verse are *Secret Destinations* (Macmillan, 1984) and an interim collection *21 Poems* (Celandine Press, 1986).   [page 38]

GILLIAN CLARKE was born in Cardiff. After reading English at University College, Cardiff she worked for the BBC in London before returning to Wales to raise a family and now lives in Cardiganshire. She began writing poetry in 1970 and was Editor of the *Anglo-Welsh Review*, 1975–84, and Writer-in-Residence at St David's University College, Lampeter, 1984–5. Publications include *The Sundial* (Gwasg Gomer, 1978), *Letter from a far country* (Carcanet, 1982) and *Selected and New Poems* (Carcanet, 1985).
                                                                                      [page 116]

WENDY COPE lives in London and works as a teacher and free-lance writer. Her first full-length collection of poems, *Making Cocoa for Kingsley Amis*, has recently been published by Faber.   [page 98]

KEVIN CROSSLEY-HOLLAND is a poet, writer for children, broadcaster and interpreter of the northern world. A regular presenter of *Time for Verse* (including a series live from the Tate based on this anthology), his 1986 publications include his fourth collection of poems, *Waterslain* (Century Hutchinson), a Poetry Book Society summer recommendation and *The Oxford Book of Travel Verse*. He is married, with two adult sons and a three-year-old daughter, and lives in Suffolk.   [page 52]

CAROL ANN DUFFY lives in London. Her most recent collection of poetry is *Standing Female Nude* (Anvil Poetry Press, 1985) and last Christmas Turret Books published a limited edition of new poems, *Thrown voices*. She has just completed a season as Visiting Writing Fellow at the North Riding College, Scarborough. [page 106]

D.J. ENRIGHT taught for many years, chiefly in the Far East, and subsequently worked in publishing in London. His *Collected Poems* came out in 1981, and his most recent collection of verse is *Instant Chronicles* (1985). He was awarded the Queen's Gold Medal for Poetry in 1981. [page 30]

GAVIN EWART the veteran British poet, was born in 1916. He has worked as a salesman, a publisher and an advertising copywriter, as well as for the British Council. His first poems were published in 1933, in magazines. *The Collected Ewart 1933–1980* (Hutchinson) was published in 1980. His latest book is *The young Pobble's Guide to His Toes* (Century Hutchinson, 1985). *The Learned Hippopotamus* (children's verse) will appear this summer. [page 18]

Note: The room with the Whistler frescoes is now the restaurant. There is no tea-room but a self-service cafeteria serving food and drink (including wine).

U.A. FANTHORPE is a 'late beginner in most things'. She started writing when she stopped teaching after sixteen years and now works as a clerk/receptionist in a Bristol hospital. Three collections of her poetry have been published by Peterloo Poets and a King Penguin Selection will appear in 1986. She was recently Arts Council Writer Fellow at St Martin's College, London. [page 62]

VICKI FEAVER was born in Nottingham in 1943 and studied at Durham University and University College, London. Her collection of poems *Close Relatives* was published by Secker and Warburg in 1981; she is currently working on a second collection and a book about Stevie Smith. She earns a living as television subtitler for Oracle Teletext and as a visiting poetry teacher for schools in London and Kent. She has four children and lives in Brixton. [page 134]

ALISON FELL was born and brought up in Scotland, and studied sculpture at Edinburgh Art College. She has worked in mixed media theatre, in Women's Centres, and as a journalist on publications including *Spare Rib*. She has been Writer in Residence in two London Boroughs, and now teaches creative writing in adult education. She has read poetry widely at venues throughout the UK. Publications include a children's novel *The Grey Dancer* (Collins/Fontana), *Every Move You Make*, an adult novel (Virago, 1984) and a poetry collection, *Kisses for Mayakovsky*, also with Virago.   [page 70]

ROY FISHER's writing has strong links with music and visual art. He works regularly as a pianist, and founded, with Lol Coxhill and Adrian Mitchell, the performing group *Jazz Duets and Poetry*; his translations of two Schubert song-cycles have been recorded by Shura Gehrman. He has published collaborations with the artists Derrick Greaves, Ronald King, Ian Tyson and Tom Phillips. His *Poems 1955–1980* is published by Oxford University Press, as is his new long poem, *A Furnace*.   [page 33]

DAVID FROMMER was born in Brussels in 1978. He has a twin sister. His favourite pastimes are modelling with Lego and writing stories. The books he likes best are the Tintin stories and Roald Dahl's children's stories. He enjoys travelling and has been to several countries in Europe and to the United States. He wrote the poem in this collection whilst waiting to go on a Tate Gallery children's tour.   [page 148]

DAVID GASCOYNE was born in 1916 and educated at Salisbury Cathedral Choir School and Regent Street Polytechnic Secondary. His first collection of poems was published in 1932, followed by *A Short Survey of Surrealism* (1935), and *Poems 1937–42*, illustrated by Graham Sutherland, was published during the war. *Collected Poems* (including *Night Thoughts*, commissioned and broadcast by the BBC in 1954) was published in 1964 and is now in its sixth printing (1984). Prewar *Journals*, published in 1978 and 1980, appeared in French translation in 1984. David Gascoyne spent about fifteen years in France where he frequented, among other painters, the studios of Hélion, Masson and Dubuffet.   [page 108]

MICHAEL HAMBURGER is a poet and translator. Born in Berlin in 1924 he emigrated to England in 1933. His own collections of poetry include *Flowering Cactus* (1950), *Weather and Season* (Longmans, 1963), and *Ownerless Earth: New and Selected Poems* (Carcanet, 1973), and his many distinguished translations include *The Poems of Gunter Grass* (1969), and *Friedrich Hölderlin: Poems and Fragments* (Routledge & Kegan Paul, 1967, new enlarged edition Cambridge University Press, 1980). His *Collected Poems* was published in 1984 by Carcanet. He was awarded the European Translation Prize in May 1985. [page 122]

JOHN HEATH-STUBBS was born in London in 1918 and read English at Queen's, Oxford. He has held visiting professorships in Alexandria, Egypt and Ann Arbor, Michigan, lectured in English at St Mark & St John, Chelsea, 1962–72, and is now a part-time tutor at Merton, Oxford. He received the Queen's Gold Medal for Poetry in 1973. He has published numerous books of verse, translations, plays and criticism and his most recent volume, *The Immolation of Aleph*, was published by Carcanet in 1985. [page 24]

JEREMY HOOKER, a former Senior Lecturer in English at the University College of Wales, Aberystwyth and creative-writing fellow at Winchester School of Art, 1981–3, is now a free-lance writer and lecturer. His selected poems, *A View from the Source*, was published in 1982, and his critical writings include studies of David Jones and John Cowper Powys, and a book of essays, *Poetry of Place*. He collaborated with Norman Ackroyd on *Itchen Water*, a book of poems and etchings, published by Winchester School of Art Press in 1982. [page 86]

Note: The dark green in the painting, together with the woman's bowed figure, gave me a powerful sense of pressure downwards, of physical and emotional gravity. Against this sombre, oppressive force, the face of the sick child was, in tone and weight, the only light – a death-light, especially in the moon of the skull, but also a light endowed with love and pity. Looking closely at the painting, and knowing something of Munch's biography, I saw him in it. Not his personal psychology alone, but the pain and darkness of the North, which he inhabited and expressed. This appeared to me in the metaphor of a dark green sea, with Munch as one who was born to it, but who was also its master. My title also refers to Munch as the sick child, the feverish boy living on in the man, who painted his dead sister and his dead mother. In painting them, he had both, in a sense, restored them to life, and revealed the North to which they all belonged. It is a personal, yet common state, where love and death are inextricably kin. I wrote not to criticise Edvard Munch, but to feel with him, and I wanted to create, in words, a kind of equivalent to what I believe he had lived, and expressed in the painting.

MICHAEL HULSE was born in Stoke-on-Trent in 1955 and studied at the University of St Andrews. He has taught at the universities of Erlangen, Eichstätt and Cologne. His poetry has taken the National Poetry Competition first prize and an Eric Gregory Award and appears from Secker & Warburg, who published his most recent collection, *Propaganda*, in 1985. [page 64]

JOHN JAMES was born in Cardiff in 1939. His publications include *Striking the Pavilion of Zero* (Ian McKelvie, 1975); *A Theory of Poetry* (Street Editions, 1977) and a poem for Bruce McLean written in response to the artist's London and Berlin exhibitions of 1983. His most recent collection of poems is *Berlin Return* (Grosseteste, 1983). [page 146]

Note: 'Lines for Richard Long' is an extract from a longer poem of the same title.

ELIZABETH JENNINGS was born in Boston, Lincolnshire in 1926 and educated at Oxford High School and St Anne's College, Oxford. Her fourteenth book of poems, *Extending the Territory*, appeared in 1985, when she was also one of the contributors to the Puffin anthology *Poets in Hand, A Quintet*. She has written a number of critical books, including *Robert Frost* and *Every Changing Shape*, and has translated Michelangelo's *Sonnets*. She has edited a number of anthologies and has given many poetry readings, in Great Britain, Florence and New York. A new *Collected Poems* will be published in 1986. [page 14]

AMRYL JOHNSON was born in Trinidad. She came to England when she was eleven and continued her education in London and later at the University of Kent. A number of her poems were published in the anthology *News for Babylon* (Chatto & Windus, 1985) and her own collection, *Long Road to Nowhere* was published by Virago Press, also in 1985. She has broadcast here and in the Caribbean and currently lives in Oxford. [page 56]

JENNY JOSEPH was born in 1932. She read English at Oxford and has worked as a lecturer, reporter and pub landlady. She now lives in Gloucestershire. Publications include *The Unlooked-for Season* (Scorpion, 1960), *Rose in the Afternoon* (J.M. Dent, 1974), *The Thinking Heart* (Secker & Warburg, 1978) and *Beyond Descartes* (Secker & Warburg, 1983). A substantial extract from a fiction called *Persephone*, in prose and verse, was published in *Argo* in November 1985 (Vol.VIII, No.1). [page 76]

SYLVIA KANTARIS, a former French tutor at Queensland University and until recently an Open University tutor, is now occupied mainly with writing and related teaching and performing activities. She lives in Cornwall. Her recent books of poetry include *The Tenth Muse* (Peterloo, 1983), *News from the Front* (co-author D.M. Thomas, Arc 1983) and *The Sea at the Door* (Secker & Warburg, 1985). [page 68]

JUDITH KAZANTZIS is a Londoner with two grown-up children. She teaches writing workshops. Her publications include *Minefield* (Sidgwick & Jackson, 1977), *The Wicked Queen* (Sidgwick & Jackson, 1980), *Touch Papers* (with two others: Allison & Busby, 1982), *Let's Pretend* (Virago Poets, 1984) and her work has also been published in magazines such as *Poetry Review*, *Ambit* and *The Honest Ulsterman*. [page 20]

Note: Originally known as 'The Bedside Farewell', the Saltonstall family portrait turns out to be more unusual than the death in childbed of one 17th-century wife. Expert dating now suggests two wives present, not one . . . the first Mrs Saltonstall died in 1630 shortly after and quite likely as a result of her third childbirth. (Her two elder and surviving children are pictured as they were at that date.)

JOHN LOVEDAY, a teacher for 35 years, was born in Norfolk in 1926. He now writes, lectures and gives readings. In the 1970s he organised a series of poetry readings and later edited an anthology for children, *Over the Bridge* (Kestrel/Puffin, 1981) of new work by poets who had participated in these readings. He has published four small poetry collections, including *Particularities* (Priapus Press, 1977) and *From the Old Foundry* (Mandeville Press, 1983). *Particular Sunlights*, a volume of selected poems, will be published by Headland in 1986. [page 74]

EDWARD LUCIE-SMITH was born in 1935 in Jamaica. He came to England in 1946 and is widely known as a poet, broadcaster, art critic and journalist. *A Tropical Childhood & other Poems* (1961) won the John Llewellyn-Rhys Memorial Prize. He has published various editions of contemporary poetry, works of art history and criticism and a volume of autobiography. [page 131]

ROGER McGOUGH, born in Liverpool and now resident in London, has three new titles for publication in 1986: *The Stowaways* (Kestrel), *Noah's Ark*, illustrated by Liljana Rylands (Fontana) and *The Kingfisher Book of Comic Verse* (Kingfisher), which he edited. [page 61]

GEORGE MACKAY BROWN has always lived in Orkney and has written several books of verse, short stories, plays, novels, children's fiction, essays, etc. Some of his work has been set to music by Peter Maxwell Davis (the opera *The Martyrdom of St. Magnus*, based on the novel *Magnus*). He is at present working on a poem-cycle. [page 104]

GERDA MAYER was born in Karlsbad, Czechoslovakia, in 1927 and came to England in 1939. Her publications include *Monkey on the Analyst's Couch*, a Poetry Book Society recommendation (Ceolfrith Press, 1980), *The Candy-Floss Tree*, an anthology for young people (with two others: Oxford University Press, 1984) and *March Postman* (a booklet from the Priapus Press, 1985). [page 26]

Note: The picture was surface cleaned in 1982 which made it altogether lighter but removed Sir B.B's rather rakish appearance. Sir Brooke Boothby is said to have been 'a minor poet, a patron of the arts, and a friend of . . . Rousseau'. He wrote poems entitled 'Sorrows' on the death of his only child Penelope who died at the age of five.

EMILY MITCHELL was born in London in 1975. She is a pupil at William Tyndale School, Islington. In 1985–6 she studied for a year in Maryland, USA. Her hobbies are swimming, skating, reading and writing poetry. [page 84]

JOHN MOLE was born in 1941. He is co-founder and editor, with Peter Scupham, of the Mandeville Press, and at present lives and works in Hertfordshire. The poem in this volume will be appearing in his next collection, *Homing*, to be published by Secker and Warburg in the Autumn of 1986. He is married to the artist Mary Norman with whom he has collaborated on a book of riddles in words and pictures, *Once There Were Dragons* (Deutsch, 1979). [page 50]

EDWIN MORGAN was born in Glasgow in 1920 and served with the Royal Army Medical Corps from 1940 to 1946. Until 1980 he was Professor of English at Glasgow University. Books of poetry include *The Second Life* (1968), *From Glasgow to Saturn* (1973), *The New Divan* (1977), *Colour Poems* (1978), *Poems of Thirty Years* (1982), *Sonnets from Scotland* (1984) and *Selected Poems* (1985). [page 138]

BLAKE MORRISON was born in Skipton, Yorkshire in 1950. He is Deputy Literary Editor of the *Observer* and author of *The Movement* (1980), *Seamus Heaney* (1982) and of a book of poems, *Dark Glasses* (Chatto & Windus, 1984). Awards and prizes include the Eric Gregory Award (1980), Somerset Maugham Award and Dylan Thomas Prize (1985).
[page 128]

PAUL MULDOON was born in 1951 in County Armagh, Northern Ireland and he has lived in Belfast since 1969. He now works for BBC Northern Ireland as a radio and television producer. His books of poetry are *New Weather* (1973), *Mules* (1977), *Why Brownlee Left* (1980) and *Quoof* (1983), all published by Faber.   [page 96]

GARETH OWEN was born in Ainsdale, Lancashire. He has published two collections of poetry, *Salford Road* (Kestrel) and *Song of the City* (Fontana). His first novel *The Final Test* (Gollancz) was short-listed for the Smarties Award in 1985. He is the author of some twelve plays, hitherto unproduced and has just completed a pseudo-documentary film, *Old Country*, about a fictional country singer.   [page 66]

SARAH JANE RATHERHAM was born in 1970. She currently attends Lordswood Girls' School, Birmingham. Her interests include drama, swimming, music (she plays the clarinet and piano) and all kinds of creative writing. She hopes to go on to university and eventually to pursue a literary career.   [page 100]

PETER REDGROVE has published nine books of poetry and seven 'metaphysical thrillers'. He is also a playwright, and won the Prix Italia in 1982. He lives in Cornwall with his poet wife Penelope Shuttle with whom he co-authored *The Wise Wound*, a revolutionary study of the female fertility cycle (Paladin 1986).   [page 119]

JEREMY REED was born in Jersey. His recent books of poetry are *By the Fisheries* (1984) and *Nero* (1985), both published by Jonathan Cape. He received an Eric Gregory Award in 1983 and in 1985 was the joint winner of the Somerset Maugham Award. Penguin are to publish his Selected Poems in 1986.   [page 110]

DAVID RODGER was born in 1935. He was educated in Northumberland and Fife and read French and German at St Andrews. He joined the British Museum in 1960 and is now an administrator for the British Library's new building project at St Pancras. His main interests are art nouveau book design, early twentieth-century poetry and Japan.

[page 141]

VERNON SCANNELL was born in 1922. During the Second World War he served with the Gordon Highlanders. In 1960 he received the Heinemann Award for Literature and in 1974 the Cholmondeley Poetry Prize. Recent publications (all from Robson Books) include *New and Collected Poems* (1980), *Winterlude* (1982) and *Ring of Truth*, a novel (1983), and his autobiographical *The Tiger & the Rose* was reprinted in 1984.

[page 47]

PETER SCUPHAM was born in Liverpool in 1933, educated at the Perse and Emmanuel College, Cambridge. He is married with four children, and lives in Hertfordshire where he runs, with John Mole, the Mandeville Press, a Private Press for the publication of new poetry. Oxford University Press will be publishing his sixth collection, *Out Late*, in 1986.

[page 28]

RUTH SILCOCK is a social worker and lives in Oxfordshire. Her poems have appeared in various journals and anthologies and a collection of poems is being published by Anvil Press later this year. She has also written several books for children.   [page 72]

ELEANOR SNOW was born in 1979. She began her education at Ackroyd Community Nursery and Ivydale School. The thing she enjoys most is playing the big drum in her music teacher's house. She especially enjoys company. Her home is in South East London where she lives with her parents and two older sisters.   [page 102]

ANNE STEVENSON is American but has lived in Britain since 1964. Her five collections of poetry include *Correspondences* and *The Fiction-Makers* (Oxford University Press), a Poetry Book Society choice for 1985. A *Selected Poems* is forthcoming in 1986.

[pages 124 & 126]

Note: Poems after Francis Bacon are from a cycle of poems on works by the artist.

GEORGE SZIRTES was born in Budapest in 1948 and came to England as a refugee in 1956. He trained as a painter – Chagallian, for want of a more accurate description – at Leeds, and has published four books of poetry, the most recent of which, *The Photographer in Winter*, is a Poetry Book Society Recommendation for Spring 1986.

[page 91]

CHARLES TOMLINSON was born in Stoke-on-Trent, educated at Cambridge, and is now Professor of English at Bristol University. He has published fifteen books of poetry with Oxford University Press, most recently *Translations* (1983), *Notes from New York* (1984) and in 1985 *Collected Poems* and *Eden*, a collection of poems and graphics (Redcliffe Press, 1985). Two cassettes of him reading are available from Keele University who are making a complete recording of his poems for their archives.   [page 88]

JOHN WAIN was born in Stoke-on-Trent, Staffordshire, in 1925. Poet, novelist, short story writer, dramatist, literary and social critic, biographer and autobiographer, he has been a professional writer for thirty years and has received several prizes and awards. From 1973–8 he was Professor of Poetry at Oxford University and was made a CBE in 1984.   [page 40]

DAVID WRIGHT was born in Johannesburg in 1920, and was Gregory Fellow in Poetry at Leeds from 1965–7. Recent publications include *To the Gods the Shades*, a volume of new and collected poems (Carcanet, 1976) and a verse translation of Chaucer's *Canterbury Tales* (Oxford University Press).   [page 54]